LASTING CHANGE

FROM THE INSIDE OUT

BY
GREGORY DICKOW

REAL. FAST. LASTING. CHANGE.

Lasting Change
From the Inside Out

For information, please write

Gregory Dickow Ministries,
P.O. Box 7000
Chicago, IL 60680

or visit us online at *www.changinglives.org.*

TABLE OF CONTENTS

INTRODUCTION

A Life-Changing Journey

Like many things in life, the idea of "fasting from wrong thinking" was borne out of frustration. I like to call it Divine Frustration. It's that feeling inside of us that says, "I'm tired of the way things have been, and I absolutely refuse to live like this any longer." I was frustrated in my own life and in what I saw in countless others lives—trying to change but getting little, if any results.

This devotional —*Lasting Change From the Inside Out*— is a part of a revolutionary concept that has unlocked the secret to true and lasting change in the lives of every-day people like you and me.

It's been said to take 6 weeks to form a good habit or break a bad one. That's why I believe the Lord put on my heart to call people to this revolutionary system of change called Fasting From Wrong Thinking. It's a 40 day journey of changing your thinking which changes your life.

Whether it's change you need in your emotions, your relationships, your finances, your body or your habits, it all begins right here: in your thinking.

This is, in my experience, the simplest and most powerful way to experience real, lasting change.

A man or woman who conquers his/her thought life, cannot be conquered.

Day 1
"If Things Were Different, I Could Really Succeed."

Today, we begin a 40-day journey of "fasting" from wrong thinking, "fasting" from failure to success, fasting from mediocrity to greatness. We will eliminate mentalities of failure and adopt mentalities of success. Fasting from wrong thinking begins with believing that: As a man thinks, so is he. So, let's THINK God's way and experience His success.

Today we're fasting from the thought that says: "If things were different, I could really succeed."

We dream of what we would do IF... if I had a better education; if I wasn't tied down to this mortgage; if the economy was better; if people treated me better; if God would come through for me; etc. Notice the common thread of failure: IF.

CHANGE IT TODAY

1. **Drop the "IF".** Stop waiting for things to get better before you make them better. Give up the excuse of "if only." "If only I had this, or if only I had that."

2. **FACE life as it is. But don't ACCEPT it as it is.** The four friends of the paralytic couldn't find a way in the house because of the crowd (Mark 2:4). So they went up on the roof. They found a way where there was no way. They didn't accept life as it was, but faced life as it was with their faith, and experienced the power of God.

3. **Recognize YOU HOLD the power to do something with your life**, regardless of the economy, your upbringing, or your past mistakes. God has given you SEED to plant (your words, your choices, your money, etc.). Begin each day sowing a seed of faith, joy, love or hope. You have a smile—use it. You have a mouth to speak God's Word, to declare His praise—do it.

4. **Don't wait for the perfect conditions.** Ecclesiastes 11:4 "He who watches the wind will not sow and he who looks at the clouds will not reap." Don't wait for the stock market, or real estate or the media to get better, before you do what you know to do. Make your life better by sowing the right seeds, beginning TODAY. Make good choices TODAY.

5. **FORGET NONE OF HIS BENEFITS.** Focus on the good you already have, what God HAS already done. Psalm 103:2-4—He forgives all. He heals all. He redeems us from all destruction. The old hymn says: "For He has done great things. He has done great things. Bless His Holy Name!"

THINK IT & SAY IT

I don't need things to be different before I succeed. I will make them different. I have the power to sow the seeds of a better life. I will not just accept whatever life brings. I will face it with faith and find a way through it. I will remember what God has done. He pardons all my sins. He heals all my diseases. He crowns me with victory. He satisfies my life with good things, so that my youth, vitality and outlook on life is refreshed and renewed, in Jesus' Name.

Day 2

THE SURVIVAL MENTALITY

Today we're going to fast from what I call the "survival mentality."

"If I can just pay my bills..."; "If I can just get my work done..."; "If I can just keep my job..."; "If I can just get through this...". These all seem like reasonable goals, but the fact is, they are born from a "survival" mentality. They position us to merely eke out a self-centered existence, rather than living the abundant life God created us to live. They set our sights too low to make a difference in anyone else's life or in the world.

YOU ARE NOT JUST A SURVIVOR—YOU ARE MORE THAN A CONQUEROR and A GIFT TO THIS WORLD.

CHANGE IT TODAY

1. **Start with the end in mind.** Proverbs 29:18 says, "Without a vision, the people run aimlessly." Develop in your mind a vision of victory, favor and blessing EVERY DAY. Begin to see yourself blessed, so that you can be a blessing (Genesis 12:1-3).

2. **See yourself as a gift to the world**—a blessing and a problem-solver to others (1 Peter 4:10).

3. **Expect abundance.** Just having "enough to get by" is small-minded, and prevents you from being a blessing to others. (John 10:10)

4. **Have the right mental attitude toward people.** When you truly care about what is best for them, you will succeed. It's easy to smile when you want the best for someone else. It's easy to sell when you're trying to bless them.

5. **Put others first.** Truly want the best for the people in 'your world.' In tough times, it's easy to pull back and focus on taking care of self. But God's system works otherwise. In Genesis 13:8-17, Abraham put Lot, first. By doing so, God blessed Abraham—more than he could contain!

6. **ADD value to others.** Ask God to put a burning desire in your heart to make other people's lives better (not as a 'people-pleaser', but as a gift to their lives). When you do, you'll never lack a good job, successful business or healthy relationships!

THINK IT & SAY IT

I thank God that I have a vision for my life. I am not surviving, I am thriving. I see myself blessed so that I can be a blessing. I am a gift to those around me. I add value to their lives, by seeking God's best for them. God has put in me the desire to love and serve others unselfishly. As I do, I will never be without. God's blessings will come upon me and overtake me, in Jesus' Name.

Day 3

"I Haven't Done Enough To Get God To Answer My Prayers Or Bless Me."

Today we're "fasting" from the thought that says: I haven't done enough to get God to answer my prayers or bless me.

When things don't go our way, we sometimes have this nagging thought that we're not holy enough or there's too much wrong in our lives to 'qualify' for God's blessing or favor.

Today we're letting go of this destructive mindset. We're ridding ourselves of a "merit-based" relationship with God.

All our lives we were told, 'you get what you deserve.' Well, the truth is, we all deserve judgment and hell. BUT GOD! (Don't you love those two words?!!!!!) Ephesians 2: BUT GOD being rich in mercy...doesn't give us what we deserve...

CHANGE IT TODAY

1. **We get what Jesus deserves!** Romans 8:17 says we are joint-heirs with Jesus Christ! His inheritance is ours. 1 John 4:17 says, "As He is, so are we in this world." We deserved the curse, but we get the blessing (Galatians 3:13).

2. **Be COVENANT-MINDED.** You have a covenant with God (Hebrews 8:12-13). A covenant is a contract. In this case, it is a contract that is guaranteed by the shed blood of Jesus Christ.

3. **Have confidence in God, not in yourself**
   (1 John 3:20-21). Confidence and faith are what draw answered prayer to our lives.

4. **Reject condemnation.** It is our heart that condemns us (for our mistakes and shortcomings). When we feel condemned, we lose confidence. Then we can't receive from God (Hebrews 10:35).

5. **Accept your freedom in Christ.** Romans 8:1: There is no condemnation for those who are in Him. If you're born-again, you are IN HIM!

6. **Be GRACE-minded.** Grace is: God giving us what we don't deserve. Hebrews 4:16 says, "Come boldly and receive mercy and grace in your time of need."

THINK IT & SAY IT

I let go of the mindset that I'm not holy enough or haven't done enough to receive from God. I receive His promises by faith. I am a joint heir with Jesus Christ. I expect to get what He deserves, not what I deserve. I have a covenant with God, and therefore I have confidence He will hear me and answer. There is no condemnation in Him. I receive His grace, freely and lavishly, in Jesus' Name.

Day 4

"WHAT IF I DON'T MAKE IT?"

Today we're fasting from the thought that says: "What if I don't make it?" "What if I don't make it through this financial trouble?" "What if I don't make it through this sickness?" "What if I don't make it through this trial?"

We must eliminate this from our thought life, and our vocabulary. Even if you rarely think this, it's a mindset that the devil subtly uses to suggest the possibility of failure.

CHANGE IT TODAY

1. **Realize, you've already made it!** If you're a child of God, you are going to live forever. Sometimes, PERSPECTIVE is all we need to take the pressure off of our performance and temporary trial.

2. **Whatever you're facing is TEMPORARY.** 2 Corinthians 4:17 says, "For our momentary, light affliction is producing for us an eternal weight of glory far beyond all comparison." The trial is temporary. This too shall pass!

3. **You are more than a conqueror!** (Romans 8:37) THIS HAS TO PERMEATE YOUR MIND. As it does, that's what turns it into a MIND-SET that creates the life of victory.

4. **Faith always finds a way (Luke 5:19).** And JESUS is PRAYING FOR YOU that your faith will not fail (Luke 22:32).

5. **The possibility of 'not making it' is not a part of the plan!** In Jeremiah 29:11, God says, "I know the plans I have for you—FOR GOOD, and NO HARM."

6. **Rest in the fact that God will never fail you, nor forsake you (Hebrews 13:5-6).** It's like a teacher that refuses to fail a student, no matter what he's going through...that's what God is like toward us!

THINK IT & SAY IT

I am more than a conqueror. No matter what I'm going through, it is temporary. I already have the victory. And this is the victory: My Faith. My faith will not fail, because Jesus is praying for me right now (Hebrews 7:25). God will not fail me. Love will not fail me. The Holy Spirit will not fail me. I will go through the mountain, go over the mountain or move the mountain, in Jesus' Name.

Day 5
"Someone Or Something Is Missing In My Life."

Today we're fasting from the thought that says: "Someone or something is missing in my life."

This idea that something is missing is what often leads to failure, sadness and huge mistakes in our lives. It also can make us angry or bitter at someone for NOT being to us what we needed them to be.

CHANGE IT TODAY

1. **You are complete in Christ.** Colossians 2:10—in Him, you have been made complete. Complete forgiveness, complete love, and complete victory ARE YOURS TODAY.

2. **Everything you need already BELONGS TO YOU in Him.** 1 Corinthians 3:22—All things belong to you. Romans 8:32—He freely gives us all things.

3. **Embrace the peace of God in your life** (John 14:27). Jesus said, "Peace I leave with you, My peace I give unto you: not as the world giveth, give I unto you". One of the definitions for peace in scripture is NOTHING MISSING. We have His peace! THINK ON THAT.

4. **Expect God's supply.** Meditate on Philippians 4:19 which says, "My God shall supply ALL YOUR NEEDS according to His riches." It's not according to our perfection or our good works, but according to His riches.

5. **Understand that people will disappoint and fail us sometimes, but God will not.** That's why we put our hope in God! Psalm 42:11 says, Why so down cast, O my soul? Put your hope in God (not people)...the help of my countenance.

6. **Ask God to OPEN YOUR EYES to see what is already in you** (Ephesians 1:18, Ephesians 3:20). The Holy Spirit is in you. The Love of God is in you. Faith is in you. These forces of God's power are in you right now if you are born again.

THINK IT & SAY IT

I am complete in Christ. There is no good thing missing in my life. I have all things in Him. My God supplies all my needs, and I expect His supply TODAY. I have the peace of God, which delivers my heart from trouble and disappointment. Even if people let me down, my God will uphold me and help me. I have the Holy Spirit, the love of God and the gift of faith in my life. I am complete in Him, in Jesus' Name.

Day 6

"WHEN ARE SUCCESS AND PROSPERITY GOING TO COME MY WAY?"

Today we are fasting from the thought that says, "When are success and prosperity going to come my way?" This mindset is preventing true success from flowing in our lives. When we wait for it to come to us, we miss the point of what it really is.

CHANGE IT TODAY

1. **Success is NOT something we obtain.** It's something we are (Genesis 39:2). The Lord was with Joseph, so he became a SUCCESSFUL and PROSPEROUS man. Notice, prosperity was not something he had, it was something HE WAS.

2. **Just as the Lord was with Joseph, He is with you—and then some!** For Joseph, God was WITH him. For you, God is also IN you. 1 Corinthians 3:16 says, "Do you not know that you are the temple of God and that the Spirit of God dwells in you?"

3. **See the image inside of you** of a successful and prosperous person, regardless of what circumstances you find yourself in. Joseph saw himself prosperous, and therefore HELPING OTHER PEOPLE SUCCEED was not a threat to him. He knew who he was.

4. **You have a treasure in you** (2 Corinthians 4:7). We have this treasure in earthen vessels. Don't doubt the treasure in you. You have power, love and a sound mind. You have wisdom, faith and joy. The kingdom of God is IN you, etc.

5. **Remember what Jesus said: "The greatest among you is the servant of all"** (Matthew 23:11). Understand that this starts with KNOWING THERE IS GREATNESS IN YOU. Serving doesn't make you great. But when you realize the greatness God put in you, you will serve others gladly. When you are secure in your own success (on the inside, because God is with you and in you), you neither feel inferior nor superior to others; you're just happy to serve.

Failure can only come when we try to find success somewhere other than in us. God put it there.

THINK IT & SAY IT

I don't need to wait for success to come my way. I am a prosperous and successful person, because God is with me AND in me. Wherever I go, I bring success. To prosper is not something I do, it's something I am. Regardless of my circumstances, success is in me. I will not wait for someone to give it to me. I have a treasure inside of me. That treasure makes me secure and confident so that I can freely and gladly serve others and see them become successful, in Jesus' Name.

Day 7

"I'M WORRIED ABOUT MY FINANCES AND WHAT'S GOING ON IN THE WORLD."

Today we are fasting from the thought that says: "I'm worried about my finances and what's going on in the world."

Crisis hotlines and therapists are being flooded by the increase of anxiety, particularly over finances. There is an obvious connection between financial distress and emotional stress, depression, insomnia, migraines, and increased suicidal thoughts. Whether you are affected by the economy or not, ANXIETY MUST GO.

CHANGE IT TODAY

1. **Know that God wants to take care of you, and take the care off your mind.** Cast your care on Him. How? Tell Him what you're anxious about. Ask Him to take care of it. Remind Him that He promised that He would. Praise Him for the answer. THEN, think only thoughts that are good, filled with expectation, faith and the answers God will give (that's my paraphrase of Philippians 4:6-8).

2. **Believe that He will supply ALL your needs** (Philippians 4:19). Sometimes, it's not "money" we need to solve a "money" problem. We need wisdom, ideas and insight. God will provide, whatever the need is. Trust Him and expect.

3. **Ask God for wisdom** (James 1:5). The Bible also says that wisdom is MORE VALUABLE THAN silver and gold

(Proverbs 8:11, Proverbs 3:15). Ask God for it, and believe you have received it.

4. **Meditate on the people of scripture whom God provided for.** In Psalm 37:25, David said, "I was young, but now I am old, and I have NEVER seen the righteous forsaken or His children begging for bread." Also, Genesis 24:1, which says "and the Lord blessed Abraham in ALL THINGS." Expect this blessing in all things in your life. Why? Because you are the seed of Abraham! (Galatians 3:29)

5. **ASK GOD TO PROSPER YOU.** Be specific. Psalm 118:25 says, "O Lord, I beseech You, send prosperity now."

6. **See yourself as irresistible.** That may sound strange, but you are fearfully and wonderfully made. Expect that people will want to hire you, keep you, or buy from your business. As a child of God, you have love, faith and power on the INSIDE of you. You are made in the image of God. See yourself that way. You have what people need. Believe it. You have not been given the spirit of fear (2 Timothy 1:7).

7. **BELIEVE IN THE CREATIVITY OF GOD.** He is not limited to meeting our needs with just money or our job. He provided water out of a rock, manna out of heaven, and fish from an empty lake! He is Jehovah Jireh—our Provider (Genesis 22:8).

THINK IT & SAY IT

I surrender my specific anxious thoughts to God. I believe God cares about my every need and wants to meet ALL my needs. I may have a need, but He has a supply! I thank Him for the answer, and I think on all the good He has done and will do in my life.

I receive the wisdom of God, and expect that wisdom to empower me more than silver or gold. I receive the prosperity and provision of God.

I am VALUABLE, because I am fearfully and wonderfully made. I have the blessing and gifts of God on the INSIDE of me. I have what people need, therefore I will always be in demand.

I believe God has countless ways to meet my needs, and I thank Him for providing, in Jesus' Name.

Day 8

"How Could I Ever Recover From This Loss?"

Today we're fasting from the thought that says: "How could I ever recover from this loss?"

We've all lost something at one time or another in our lives. If it hasn't been money, it's been time or relationships, opportunity or HOPE. Well today, we begin to GET IT BACK!

We must abstain from the thoughts that say, "we can't recover"; "we'll never know great days like we did in the past"; or "I've lost too much to recover".

CHANGE IT TODAY

1. **Let this thought permeate your mind:** God is a God of restoration. Joel 2:25-26 says "I will the restore the years that have been lost." Whether it's the stock market, bad decisions, what others have done to you, God will restore.

2. **Get rid of the mentality of "settling."** We must refuse to settle. The 10 lepers wouldn't settle for their leprosy; they cried out to Jesus. The woman with the demon-possessed daughter wouldn't take no for an answer. Bartimeus wouldn't stop shouting until he recovered his sight. REFUSE to settle for the way it is.

3. **Realize God WANTS you to go to Him and ask Him to avenge you.** In Luke 18, the unjust judge avenged the widow because of her persistence. HOW MUCH MORE WILL GOD AVENGE HIS CHILDREN!!!!!! (Luke 18:6-7)

4. **All the promises of God are YES** (2 Corinthians 1:20). He has promised restoration and recovery, so ask Him for it TODAY. God wants you to recover more than you do. Believe this.

5. **Believe the promise:** the thief has to repay 7-fold of what he's stolen (Proverbs 6:31). The thief = the devil, time, the economy, fear. These are all thieves that you can expect to give back, supernaturally, what has been lost in your life.

6. **Re-position your thinking for expectation.** Ephesians 3:20 says He is able to do "far over and above all that we [dare] ask or think [infinitely beyond our highest prayers, desires, thoughts, hopes, or dreams]". Pray, ask, think, dream, desire and hope HIGHER.

7. **Expect recovery!** "You shall surely overtake your enemies and you shall recover all." (1 Samuel 30:8)

THINK IT & SAY IT

I will recover all that has been lost in my life. I expect the restoration of lost relationships, lost money, lost hope and lost opportunities. I will not settle for loss and lack. God will avenge me. He will restore. I ask Him and expect Him to avenge me of all that has been lost in my life. I call forth a seven-fold return of what has been taken from me, in Jesus' Name.

Day 9
"THE PROBLEM-FOCUSED MENTALITY"

Today we're fasting from what I call the "problem-focused" mentality. And we're going to begin to think with a "solution-focused" mentality.

What I mean by this is simply: you must choose to live life as a problem solver, not a problem 'reporter'. It's one thing to 'report' the news, but it's another to MAKE the news. The problem-mentality just reports the problem. The solution-mentality solves the problem. Winston Churchill said, "A pessimist sees the difficulty in every opportunity; an optimist sees the opportunity in every difficulty."

CHANGE IT TODAY

1. **Never be satisfied with just recognizing a problem.** There are enough critics and complainers in the world. The world needs 'solution-minded' people, not just those who can report a problem.

2. **We are compensated in life for the problems we solve,** not the problems we merely recognize. Joseph not only recognized the famine coming, he found a solution for the famine (Genesis 41:25-41). As a result, he became the most powerful man in the world, and the wealthiest. Even Pharaoh bowed his heart to Joseph and recognized his power and authority (Genesis 45:8).

3. **Love Math!** What do I mean? Mathematics is a great discipline because it PROVES there is a solution to

5:40 - mark

every problem. Whether you liked math in school or not, we need to get this: there is a solution to EVERYTHING. Look for it.

4. **You have the mind of Christ** (1 Corinthians 2:16). With His mind, you will find His solutions. Every problem man created, God had a solution and turned it into an opportunity. Romans 8:28—He will make all things work together for good FOR YOU, who love God and are called to His purpose.

5. **Lean on the Holy Spirit.** As we are led by the Holy Spirit and pray in the Holy Spirit, we bring His solutions into our situation. Romans 8:26-27 says, "...The Spirit helps our weaknesses. For we do not know how to pray as we should, but the Spirit Himself makes intercession for us with groanings too deep for words. Now He who searches the hearts knows what the mind of the Spirit is, making intercession for us according to the will (solutions) of God."

6. **Stop talking ABOUT the problem, and start talking to it.** The solution begins by talking TO, not talking about. Jesus said, "if you shall say TO this mountain, be removed and cast into the sea, and do not doubt...it shall obey you" (Mark 11:23). Use your mouth to move the mountain.

THINK IT & SAY IT

I choose the "solution" mentality, and give up the "problem" mentality. I believe God will give me the interpretations to life's problems, and will bless me with wisdom and answers. I believe there is a solution to every problem, and because I have the mind of Christ, I will find the solution. I welcome the Holy Spirit to pray through me and bring God's will and solutions to my life and those around me, in Jesus' Name.

Day 10

THE PROBLEM-FOCUSED MENTALITY, PART 2

Today we are continuing to fast from the 'problem-focused' mentality.

Yesterday, there was so much I wanted to share that I decided to split it up and share the rest today. You can look at life through a 'problem' lens or a 'solution' lens. If you're looking for problems, you will find them. And if you're looking for solutions, you will find them. Decide where to place your focus. Let's shift our focus onto solutions. As we change our thinking, we will change our world!

CHANGE IT TODAY

1. **Stop fighting shadows.** Shadows (of fear and worry, sickness and doubt, etc.) leave when light comes. God saw darkness (Genesis 1:2) BUT said "Light." It was the light that cast out the darkness. Psalm 119:130 says, "the entrance of His word brings light". As you shine the light of God's Word on the 'shadow', or your problem, it will leave.

2. **Ask God for wisdom.** James 1:5 says, "If any man lacks wisdom, let him ask of God who gives to all men generously..." God is filled with solutions for any and every situation we face.

3. **Expect solutions.** The stream of wisdom that is available to you is unleashed when you EXPECT answers and expect wisdom. Be solution-oriented in everything. Expect to receive. Acts 3:5.

4. **See your crisis as an opportunity.** In the Chinese alphabet, the character for "CRISIS" is exactly the

same character for "OPPORTUNITY." You can see a challenge as a crisis that produces fear and worry, OR as an opportunity that produces energy, imagination, and faith.

5. **Train your mind to look for solutions and you WILL STOP complaining.** Instead of just trying to stop complaining by being "holy" enough, let's change what we're thinking. As you LOOK for solutions in every situation, you WILL stop complaining.

6. **See the 'problem' you're facing, as the pathway to your promotion.** Once you solve it, you'll be one step closer to God's greatness for your life. You'll have proven to yourself that you can't be beat. You'll inspire your faith and discover that God equipped you to face any challenge, and you will win.

THINK IT & SAY IT

I am a problem solver. I ask for and receive wisdom today to overcome the problems I face. I have the light of God's Word bringing light to every situation. Shadows of death, darkness, fear and lack, LEAVE my life today. I embrace the opportunity to overcome what is right in front of me, and step into God's promotion for my life. I look for and expect solutions today, in Jesus' Name.

Day 11
THE SCARCITY MENTALITY

Today we are fasting from a "scarcity mentality."

The 'scarcity' or 'poverty' mentality says, "There's just not enough for everybody." It's a mentality that also thinks: "Someone else's success is a threat to my own", or my success is a threat to others." This is nonsense. This is what causes greed, jealousy and unhealthy competition. When we think 'there isn't enough,' we become stingy and reluctant to give. As a result, we paralyze our own harvests.

CHANGE IT TODAY

1. **The earth is abundant, and always will be.** We have NOT depleted this earth. For example, I recently read that there are huge coal mines on certain Indian territories, where they are finally considering mining. Great wealth is still in this earth. Psalm 24:1 says, "The earth is the Lord's and the FULLNESS thereof". Notice: FULLNESS, not emptiness.

2. **There is a seed in every harvest.** Yes, that's what I meant! Of course, we know there is a harvest in every seed. But we need to realize we will never run out of seeds, which will always perpetuate harvests.

3. **God is reserving treasures for you.** "I will give you the treasures of darkness. And hidden wealth of secret places, so that you may know that it is I,The LORD, the God of Israel, who calls you by your name" (Isaiah 45:3).

4. **Stop thinking your success deprives others OR that others' success deprives you.** We need to realize in a DEEP way, that being blessed is infinitely more

beneficial to others, than us not being blessed. It empowers us to be a blessing. We have to begin believing there is enough for us, AND for those around us. No one HAS to be deprived of joy, abundance, and successful relationships.

5. **As He is, so are we in this world** (1 John 4:17). Jesus fed MULTITUDES, not just a few. He healed EVERYONE who touched Him—Mark 3:10. He found money in fishes' mouths. He turned 5 loaves and 2 fish into an all-you-can-eat buffet for 5000 men! He always knew there was enough. When He fed the multitudes, they ate as MUCH AS THEY WANTED, and then there was plenty left over (John 6:12-13).

THINK IT & SAY IT

Abundant blessing is always available for me. I will always have a supply, because I will always have seeds to sow. I expect the treasures of God to show up in my life beginning today. My success deprives no one except the devil! I am blessed to be a blessing. The anointing to meet an abundance of needs is in me, in Jesus' Name!

Day 12

"I Don't Have"

Today we're fasting from the thought that says:
"I don't have...."

I don't have the right job, the right relationships, the education I need, the money I need, the happiness I need, etc. And the hits just keep on rolling.

I am convinced that the more we focus on what we don't have in life, the more we will miss out on. The more we focus on what we do have, the more will be attracted to us.

CHANGE IT TODAY

1. **Change the cycle of thinking from "what do I need" TO "what do I have."** We all have needs, but dwelling on them, doesn't meet them. A mindset that "I have a lot," will strengthen you emotionally, and empower you practically.

2. **Embrace the good in your life.** As hard as this is in tough times, we must focus on what we have. Psalm 103:2 says, "Forget none of His benefits—who pardons ALL your sins, heals ALL your diseases..." David was continually attacked by enemies, but his defense included remembering what God had already done.

3. **Ask God to open your eyes.** Surrounded by enemy armies, Elisha's servant became afraid. Elisha's prayer was "Lord, open the eyes of your servant, to see that there are more for us than those against us...and he saw!" (2 Kings 6:17) He didn't pray for MORE help, but rather to SEE the help he already had.

ing to get your needs met. Give thanks for
e has done. 10 lepers were cleansed. One
back and thanked Jesus. This one was made
. See? He didn't thank God so he could get
He just thanked God, AND MORE CAME
17:12-19).

5. **Change how you read your Bible.** Don't read it to get
something. Read it to DISCOVER 'whatchya' already
got (Philemon 6; Ephesians 1:3)!

THINK IT & SAY IT

I choose to focus on what I have. I have treasure in me. I
have the power of God in me. I embrace the good that
God has already done. I thank God that my eyes are en-
lightened to see what is for me, and what is in me, and I will
thank God for what He has already done. From this day forward I will read the Bible to discover what I already have, in
Jesus' Name!

Day 13
"THIS IS TOO MUCH PRESSURE; TOO MANY TRIALS"

Today we're fasting from the thought that says: "This is too much pressure, too many trials, too much for me to take."

With all that's going on in our lives and our world, we often wish it would all just stop. We need to look at pressure, trials and problems in a WHOLE NEW WAY.

CHANGE IT TODAY

1. **Today, start seeing the pressure in your life as a blessing!** I'm not saying to lay down and take whatever life or the devil brings. But it's the hottest fires that make the hardest steel. You are becoming strong!

2. **Realize you're not alone.** The apostle Paul was so overwhelmed by the pressure around him that he wanted to just end his life (2 Corinthians 1:8-10).

3. **Discover the silver lining.** Paul discovered it and said things were so bad in his life, that "we expected to die. BUT AS A RESULT, we stopped relying on ourselves and learned to rely ONLY on God, who raises the dead (2 Corinthians 1:9 Amplified).

4. **Intimidate the thing trying to intimidate you.** When you're up against it, declare like Paul, "this was the best thing that could have happened, because we were forced to trust God totally" (2 Corinthians 1:9 Message Translation). This scares the devil!

-hearted about your trials. James said, "Count ..." (James 1:3).

igs in perspective. Paul whimsically and ously concludes, "We were forced to trust God —NOT A BAD IDEA, SINCE HE'S THE GOD WHO RAI₅Е₅ THE DEAD!" (2 Corinthians 1:9 Message). Duh!

7. **Say of the Lord, "He is my refuge...My God, in Him I will trust"** (Psalm 91:2). Trust Him who raises the dead to rescue you! (Jeremiah 39:18 NASB).

THINK IT & SAY IT

I make up my mind to see pressure as an opportunity to trust in God completely. I will trust and not be afraid. Whatever comes against me will force me to totally trust God, and He will deliver me. I rejoice in my trials, because if God can raise the dead, He will certainly rescue me in any and every situation, in Jesus' Name.

Day 14
"AT THIS POINT, THINGS MAY NEVER CHANGE."

Today we're fasting from the thought that says: "At this point, things may never change."

Accompanying thoughts include: "Things just might not turn around for me." "They're not going to get much better."

1. **Think MIRACULOUSLY. God is a God of miracles.** (A miracle = A divine interruption of fixed natural laws and natural time.) Psalm 77:14 says, "You are the God who performs miracles; You display Your power among the peoples."

2. **God has a timing and due season for everything.** Galatians 6:9 says, "In due season, you SHALL REAP."

3. **Believe God will take everything that the devil can dish out at you, and turn it around** (Genesis 50:20). God will take what was meant for evil and turn it to good.

4. **YOU HAVE "REVERSAL OF FORTUNE" IN YOUR GENES!** Esther 9:1(b) says, "In the day that the enemies of the Jews hoped to have power over them, it was turned to the contrary!" That's your spiritual lineage (Galatians 3:29).

5. **Declare today, that things will not remain as they have been!** (Ezekiel 21:26 Amplified) God will right every wrong (Romans 12:19).

THINK IT & SAY IT

I believe in the God of miracles. He will display His power in my life. There is a due season for me, and He will make things beautiful in my life. I expect a reversal of fortunes in my favor, and I declare that things will not remain as they have been. They will get better beginning today, in Jesus' Name!

"It Is What It Is."

Today we're fasting from the thought that says: "It is what it is."

Ever heard that one? You haven't sinned if you have said it or thought it; but it's a mentality that needs to be eliminated. Stop thinking 'I have to accept it the way it is.' NO. NO. NO.

CHANGE IT TODAY

1. **Remember yesterday's scripture promise:** Ezekiel 21:26 AMP says "Things will not remain, as they have been."

2. **Embrace "IT" as God's Word says it is.** Hebrews 11:1 says, "Faith IS the substance of things hoped for..."

3. **Prophesy to "IT." When the mother's child died in Elisha's day, she DEFINED what 'it' is.** When the prophet asked her, "Is it well with the lad?", she responded, "IT IS WELL." Notice she said, "IT IS WELL", when it wasn't quite well. But "IT" took on flesh and bone, when she spoke "IT" as she believed.

4. **Think like a mountain mover. That's what you are!** "Whosoever will say to this mountain 'be uprooted and cast into the sea', IT will obey you" (Mark 11:23). Expect IT to obey you.

5. **Believe IT is getting better all the time!** Proverbs 4:18 says your path is getting brighter and brighter; better and better!

THINK IT & SAY IT

It is what God says it is! I declare that things will not remain as they have been. I prophesy to "IT" in my life and declare that IT IS WELL—no matter what. I am a mountain mover, and I expect the mountains to obey me. It is getting better and better for me every day. I am going from glory to glory, in Jesus' Name.

Day 16
"I Don't Read The Bible Enough."

Today, we're fasting from the thought that says: "I don't read the Bible enough."

Who hasn't thought that? But, it's not how MUCH you read it, but HOW you see it, and how much you BELIEVE what you do read. We must begin to look at the Bible differently...

CHANGE IT TODAY

1. **See it as a love letter from God to you!** Through these eyes, you will truly release more power in your life. Look up Deuteronomy 7:8.

2. **Knowledge puffs up, but love builds up** (1 Corinthians 8:1). Read it to discover God's love, and it will build you up!!!!!

3. **See it as a description of WHO you are in Christ, not a list of do's and don't's.** "WHO" you are will shape "WHAT" you do.

4. **Make "believing it" the goal.** Of course, I encourage you to read it consistently; but read it to get to a place of believing it. John 6:29—our job is: to believe!

5. **See it as seed.** Plant it as seed in your heart, and expect the harvest of God's promises to come Mark 4:26.

THINK IT & SAY IT

God's Word is a love letter to me. I break the mentality of guilt or condemnation for not reading it enough. My goal is to BELIEVE whatever I do read. As I do, it builds me up. I plant the seed of it in my heart, and my harvest is assured, in Jesus' Name.

Day 17

"THE WILL OF GOD IS SUCH A MYSTERY."

Today we're fasting from the thought that says: "The will of God is such a mystery." Or, "It's too hard to figure out."

Many people strive to do the will of God, only to be frustrated, and often confused. Can we ever be SURE of the will of God? We can. And I believe this will help...

CHANGE IT TODAY

1. **Change the way you look at the Bible.** Yesterday we established that we need to look at the Bible as a love letter, a description of who we are in Christ, and a collection of Divine seeds for the harvests of life.

2. **Today, you must see the Bible as a "Will".** It is God's LAST WILL & TESTAMENT (Hebrews 9:15-17). Enclosed in this book is EVERYTHING Jesus, after dying, has left to His loved ones—that's you and me!

3. **Remember, a will goes into effect when someone dies.** Hebrews 9:17 says, "because a will is in force only when somebody has died; it never takes effect while the one who made it is living." Jesus died so His 'will' could go into effect in your life.

4. **See yourself in God's will NOW.** Through Jesus' blood, God has placed us IN His will.

5. **The gospel is forgiveness AND an inheritance that now belongs to us** (Acts 26:18). Read the scriptures to discover your inheritance, and know what belongs to you NOW.

6. Now, take the pressure off yourself trying to discover what to DO, and focus on discovering what is YOURS. This will change how you look at yourself and how you live!

THINK IT & SAY IT

God has placed me in His will. I don't have to strive to find it. God's will is His covenant toward me—His promised inheritance that is mine through the blood of Jesus. I will see the Bible as God's will TOWARD me. I will read it to discover what belongs to me. His inheritance is mine, in Jesus' Name!

Day 18

"WILL I EVER BE FREE FROM THIS FINANCIAL PRESSURE?"

Today we're fasting from the thought that says, "Will I ever be free from this financial pressure?"

Let's change it today, and break free from financial pressure!

CHANGE IT TODAY

1. **Understand the power of decision.** Decide that you will deal with money the way God's Word says to (John 2:5) ...no matter what.

2. **Understand the kingdom of God.** Heaven is a place; but the kingdom of God is God's way of doing things. When you seek to do things God's way, provision comes (Matthew 6:33).

3. **Understand pressure's goal:** to get you to make a decision that temporarily relieves the pressure, even though it doesn't produce results (Luke 4:2-4). Resist this pressure by speaking the Word of God.

4. **Look outward, not inward.** Find someone worse off, and help relieve their financial pressure. You will be sowing for a supernatural harvest (Proverbs 19:17).

5. **He must increase but I must decrease** (John 3:30). As you increase your focus and attention on Jesus, pressure loses its power over you (Hebrews 12:1-3).

6. **Take spiritual inventory.** THERE ARE MORE FOR YOU THAN THOSE AGAINST YOU (2 Kings 6:15-17).

THINK IT & SAY IT

I walk in the power of the kingdom of God. I do things God's way, and I have supernatural results. I refuse to make my decisions to relieve pressure, but I make my decisions in line with the Word of God. I declare that God provides for my every need, and my decisions line up with God's Word. I fix my eyes on Jesus and trust that God has an army of angels surrounding me and helping me, in Jesus' Name.

Day 19

"I'm Afraid."

Today we're fasting from the granddaddy of all wrong thinking: "I'm afraid."

Fear is at the root of just about every negative thing that happens in our lives. We're afraid of failing, afraid of being alone or rejected, afraid of running out of money, afraid that people will let us down, afraid that we won't find a spouse, or a job, and the list goes on and on. All fear is rooted in the core belief that God's Word won't work. For example, the fear of not having enough is rooted in the fear that Philippians 4:19 isn't true. If you believe that "God will supply all your needs according to His riches..." then fear leaves.

Let's fast from the thought "I'm afraid."

CHANGE IT TODAY

1. **Meditate on the fact that God's Word is true.** In John 17:17 Jesus said, "Thy Word is truth." What God says is fact—whether or not you feel it, whether or not you see it, or whether or not you have ever experienced it.

2. **Consider God's track record.** 1 Kings 8:56 says, "Thanks be to the Lord. He has given rest to His people Israel. He has done all that He promised. Every word has come true of all His good promise, which He promised..." (New Life Version). He has done all that He has promised. He has never failed. Fear leaves when you can rely on something that can't fail. There are over 1000 predictions or prophecies in the Bible—promises that God made before they

happened. The chances of merely 17 of these coming to pass is ONE out of 450 billion x 1 billion x 1 trillion! Yet, not one of these 1000 promised have failed.

3. **Accept the truth that what we fear comes upon us.** In Job 3:25, Job feared that his children would curse God, and that's what happened. When you realize fear has the power to produce negative results, you stop dabbling in it. When a child learns what fire can do, he no longer plays with matches!

4. **Perfect love casts out fear...1 John 4:18.** Flood your mind with thoughts of love—God's love for you, what He was willing to do to rescue you. If He would die for you while you were in sin, separated from God, what wouldn't He do for you? There's just nothing He wouldn't do for you! Think on that, and fear will leave.

5. **There is a promise from God's Word for every need you will ever experience.** In fact there are over 7000 promises in the Bible. That's 7000 solutions to life's problems! For example, there is a promise of protection in Psalm 91:1-12, which delivers you from the fear of tragedy.

6. **Pause and think about the fact that God is with you.** Psalm 23:4 says, "Though I walk through the valley of the shadow of death, I will fear no evil—for YOU ARE WITH ME." God's presence is the secret to a fear-free life. All fear ultimately is a sense of God's absence, or our separation from God. By contrast, a sense of God's presence delivers us from fear. Hebrews 10:19 says we enter the holy place of His presence by the blood of Jesus. YOU ARE IN HIS PRESENCE, NOW—therefore, fear not!

THINK IT & SAY IT

God's Word is true, whether I feel it or not. He has kept all of His promises, and has never failed. Fear leaves me because I rely on something that can't fail—His promises.

What I fear comes upon me, therefore I will fear ONLY GOD, and He will come upon me! God loves me perfectly, and I will not think otherwise, no matter what!

God has made 7000 promises to me, because He knows I need them! God is with me, and therefore I will fear no evil, in Jesus' Name!

Day 20
"I Can't Control My Emotions."

Today we're fasting from the thoughts that say: "I can't control my emotions. I'm such an emotional person. My emotions get the best of me." We all have emotions, but unfortunately sometimes THEY have us!

God created us to live with positive and healthy emotions. It's the negative ones that can harm us, our relationships and our future. The idea that we are "victims" of our emotions because of our gender, our culture, our nationality, or our personality type, has to be eliminated.

CHANGE IT TODAY

1. **Our emotions are the result of our thoughts.** If you think sad thoughts, you will become sad. If you think joyful and happy thoughts, you will become happy. As a man thinks within, so is he (Proverbs 23:7).

2. **Reject the belief that your emotions are the result of your nationality.** You are made in God's image, with His likeness and His mind. As you think His Word, your emotions will follow.

3. **You have been given SELF-CONTROL.** It IS in you. 2 Timothy 1:7 says, "God has given you power, love and a sound mind (SELF-CONTROL)." Galatians 5:23 says the fruit of the spirit includes SELF-CONTROL. And the spirit is in you!

4. **Believe you are in control.** As you control your thoughts, you will control your emotions. THEN, you will not feel the urge to control others!

5. **Remember God's goodness.** Jeremiah FORGOT what happiness was, because he talked himself into misery (Lamentations 3:17). When he began to think about the goodness of God, JOY WAS RESTORED. Emotions follow thoughts, whether good or bad.

THINK IT & SAY IT

I am not under the control of my emotions any more. They are under my control. As I fill my mind with good thoughts, they will become good emotions. I can control my emotions by my thought life; and my thought life is surrendered to God's Word. I have self-control and dominion over my life. And from this day forward, my emotions serve me, rather than control me, in Jesus' Name.

Day 21

"THE THINGS AROUND ME ARE REALLY GETTING TO ME."

Today we're fasting from the thought that says: "The things around me are really getting to me."

We don't have to be moved by the world around us. There is something greater working in us!

CHANGE IT TODAY

1. **Reject the belief that your emotions and behavior are controlled by the events in your life.** Our emotions and our lives are transformed, changed and shaped by the "renewing of our minds" (Romans 12:2). Change your thoughts, and your emotions will follow.

2. **The quality of your life is not determined by what happens around you, but what happens within you.** Proverbs 4:23 says, "Watch over your heart with all diligence; for out of it flow the issues of life."

3. **Believe in the power within.** Ephesians 3:20 says God is able to do above all we ask or think BASED ON THE POWER THAT WORKS WITHIN US. 1 John 4:4 says, "Greater is He that is in you, than he that is in the world."

4. **Learn to use affliction to YOUR ADVANTAGE.** 2 Corinthians 4:17 says, "It (the momentary affliction) produces an eternal weight of glory far beyond all comparison."

5. **How? It ONLY works** "WHILE WE LOOK NOT AT THE THINGS WHICH ARE SEEN, BUT AT THE THINGS WHICH ARE NOT SEEN." That's the Word of God.

6. **Change your focus.** When you look through a viewfinder of a camera, you can place the focus on a number of different objects. It's UP TO YOU, the VIEWER. In the same way, we need to focus on WHAT GOD SAYS, and not on any of the things, even if they may seem closer to the screen! 2 Corinthians 5:7 says, "We walk by faith, not by sight."

THINK IT & SAY IT

I refuse to let the events of my life to control my emotions or my way of thinking. My life is transformed by the renewing of my mind. I believe God's power is working in me, to create a life beyond my wildest dreams. I will take advantage of anything that goes on around me by FOCUSING on what God says. As I keep my eyes on His promises, it is PRODUCING His GLORY in my life, in Jesus' Name!

Day 22
"SOMEDAY"

Today we're fasting simply from the thought: "Someday."
"Someday" I'm going to live my dream. "Someday" I'm
going to succeed. "Someday" I'm going to overcome
this problem...

It's time to stop dreaming and start doing.

CHANGE IT TODAY

1. **Think ACTION.** Procrastination is the promise of fools.
   The moment we say, "I'll start tomorrow," we are
   defeated. The secret of winning is action.

2. **Discover the difference between the baker and
   the cupbearer** (Genesis 40:1-23). Both of them had
   dreams that Joseph interpreted.

3. **NOTICE:** the baker had a basket on his head (his
   hope was only in his head). He died.

4. **Stop dreaming, start serving.** The cupbearer had a
   cup in his hand. He took action and served—He was
   promoted. Matthew 20:26 says, "The greatest among
   you is the servant of all." A servant pushes everyone
   up around him.

5. **Those who KNOW GOD, DO** (Daniel 11:32). Focus on
   knowing God better. Don't get to know religion and
   ritual. Get to know God. It will produce action in
   your life.

6. **WORK begins in your mind.** People that are lazy in life
   are first mentally lazy. Stop day-dreaming and start

day-building. See yourself doing in your mind, and you will DO in life. John 13:17 says, "If you know these things, you are blessed if you do them. James 1:22 says, "But prove yourselves doers of the word, and not merely hearers..."

7. **Believe in the power of action.** Action is the antidote to despair and sadness. Elijah broke free from despair when he rose and took action (1 Kings 19:4-14).

8. **Work with what God gave you.** Psalm 118:24 says, "THIS IS THE DAY THE LORD HAS MADE"...Maximize it! Do one thing, at least right now, toward a great goal in your life. If you don't have one, make that your one thing, now.

THINK IT & SAY IT

I have the secret of winning: action. My hope is not just in my head, it's in my hands. As I serve others, I will experience my dreams. I know my God, and I do exploits. I am blessed, because I am a doer. I will maximize this day because it's the one God made. I will seize it, in Jesus' Name.

Day 23
"WHEN I OVERCOME THIS PROBLEM, I AM REALLY GOING TO BE HAPPY."

Today we're fasting from the thought that says: **"When I overcome this problem, I am really going to be happy."** Whether the problem is a trial, a bill or a person, you can (and should) be happy BEFORE any of that changes or improves.

CHANGE IT TODAY

1. **The problem is not the problem;** It's HOW you look at it. When the disciples were in the boat, WATER was flooding their ship (Mark 4:35-42). Their focus was the water, when it should have been JESUS in the back of the boat. His presence is FULLNESS OF JOY.

2. **Happiness is NOT a state of being, but a state of THINKING.** Proverbs 23:7—As a man thinks within, so is he. There can be no doubt that a STATE OF MIND always leads to a STATE OF BEING.

3. **Happiness is LEARNED.** In Philippians 4:11, Paul said, "I have learned, in whatsoever state I am, therewith to be content." How did he learn it? He GAVE UP trying to fix everything on the outside, and embraced God's presence (Christ in him) as his source of true happiness.

4. **See your life as a gift to others.** You are more blessed (HAPPY, FORTUNATE) when you give, than when you receive (Acts 20:35).

5. **Happiness is a decision.** Someone told me recently, "when I decided to do something about being unhappy, everything began to change." It was simply their DECISION, that brought about change. Don't underestimate the power of decision (Deuteronomy 30:19).

6. **We DO need to set our minds on things above, not on this earth** (Colossians 3:2). No matter how good our lives on earth can be, It is nothing compared to the pleasures, happiness and joy we will have in heaven.

THINK IT & SAY IT

I will focus on the PRESENCE OF GOD in my life. He is with me. I fill my mind with the Word of God and it produces joy and happiness. I will not try to fix everything on the outside, but enjoy God's love, and I expect His presence to melt my mountains like wax! I choose to live life on the giving side, and I expect great reward in heaven. And I choose to be happy today, in Jesus' Name.

Day 24
"WHAT IF"

Today we're fasting from the thought that says: "WHAT IF".
What if something bad happens? What if I lose my job?
What if God doesn't help me? What if my children don't turn
out right? Stop letting the "what if" thoughts paralyze you
from trusting God and acting on His Word.

CHANGE IT TODAY

1. **Remember who you are. You are a lover of God, and
   called according to His purpose.** Romans 8:28 says,
   "All things work together for those who love God and
   are called according to His purpose." THAT'S YOU.

2. **Expect the power of God's intervention.** No matter
   what happens in life, the Scripture promises it will turn
   for your good, if you expect it to and invite the Holy
   Spirit to get involved (Romans 8:26-27).

3. **Make life happen. Rather than letting life just happen
   to you, be pro-active.** All speculation and fear
   disappear when we ACT on the Word of God. Do one
   thing in the Word of God. Give something away; pray
   for someone.

4. **Expect the best.** Jabez prayed that God would bless
   him and enlarge him. Read 1 Chronicles 4:10. WE
   HAVE A BETTER COVENANT (Read Hebrews 8:7-13).

5. **You are already blessed. Believe it.** Ephesians 1:3
   says, "He has already blessed us with all..." Also,
   Romans 8:32 says "With Jesus, He has freely given us
   all things!"

THINK IT & SAY IT

I expect the best beginning today. God has already blessed me and enlarged me. I expect His blessing to show up in my life beginning today. He will turn every negative situation around for His glory and for my good. As I act on the Word of God, I will see His blessing show up in every area of my life, in Jesus' Name!

Day 25
"I'M SO BAD AT MAKING DECISIONS..."

Today we're fasting from the thought that says: "I'm so bad at making decisions..."

OK, we're going to break out of this mindset. Here's how:

CHANGE IT TODAY

1. **You have the mind of Christ** (1 Corinthians 2:16)!

2. **Take inventory.** You've not been given a spirit of fear, but power, love and a sound mind.

3. **Trust that God can make up for a bad decision with His grace.** You have to believe this today! Proverbs 16:9 says, "Though man plans his way, the Lord directs his steps."

4. **The will of God is so much bigger than we think.** Get rid of a narrow-minded view of God's will. It's not like finding a needle in a haystack. It's much easier than that. In fact, it's like finding the haystack! Just stay in the boundaries of LOVE. If you're believing the love of God and loving others, you have fulfilled the whole law! You're in the will of God!

5. **You have the Spirit of God in you!** 1 Corinthians 2:9-10 says, "But as it is written, Eye hath not seen, nor ear heard, neither have entered into the heart of man, the things which God hath prepared for them that love him. But God hath revealed them unto us by His Spirit: for the Spirit searcheth all things, yea, the deep things of God."

6. Word-based decisions are the best decisions.

Isaiah 55:11 says the Word will not return void. Whenever you are about to decide something, be convinced about what the scripture says about it, and go with that. If you're not sure, don't be ashamed to get godly counsel from your church.

THINK IT & SAY IT

I have a sound mind, therefore I make sound decisions. I have the mind of Christ. I have the Spirit of God in me, and therefore I expect Him to reveal to me the way to go. God will direct my steps and I will trust Him. My decisions will line up with the Word of God, and will not return empty.

Day 26
"I Don't Have Enough."

I want to remind you that our "fasting" is not about food. It's about "abstaining" from something. In our case, we are abstaining or GIVING UP wrong ways of thinking.

Today I want to build upon a thought from our original 40 day Fast from Wrong Thinking:

...The thought that says, "I don't have enough..."

This thought is an invisible fence that keeps us in the back-yard of lack and deficiency.

It says, "I don't have enough money. I don't have enough time. I don't have enough friends. I don't have enough experience. I don't have enough education..."

CHANGE IT TODAY

1. **The God-of-more-than-enough lives in you.** Adjust your thinking now. ENOUGH is inside of you. JEHOVAH JIREH—The Lord, The Provider—is in you.

2. **Whatever you SEEM to not have enough of, SOW.** If you don't seem to have enough friends for example, sow friendship (Proverbs 18:24). When you give what you have, it reinforces that you BELIEVE God will provide.

3. **BELIEVE that God will give you the DESIRES of your heart** (Psalm 37:4).

4. **Meditate on the power of Jesus HANDS.** When the little boy gave his 5 loaves and 2 fish, he put it in the hands of Jesus...It was multiplied to feed 5000

John 6:1-14. Whatever seems to be lacking in your life, put in the hands of Jesus—commit to Him, and He will multiply it. Whatever His hands touched was healed, delivered and empowered.

5. **Expect the blessing of God to come upon you AND overtake you** Deuteronomy 28:2. This "blessing" is your inheritance because of the cross—Galatians 3:13.

6. **Meditate:** "I have come that you would have life in abundance, to the FULL, till it overflows."— Jesus. John 10:10b Amplified.

THINK IT & SAY IT

The God of more than enough—El Shaddai—lives in me. THEREFORE, I always have enough. My God is more than enough, and He is in me, therefore, "ENOUGH" is in me. He fills me to the full, and His blessings overtake me.

He gives back to me, good measure, pressed down, shaken together and running over, in Jesus' Name!

Day 27

"THE MENTALITY OF SELF-PITY"

Today we're fasting from the mentality of SELF-PITY. This includes thoughts such as, "Nobody cares." "Nobody notices." "What does my life matter?".

These thoughts bring progress and joy in our lives to a screeching halt.

CHANGE IT TODAY

1. **Discover J.O.Y.** (Jesus, Others, Yourself). As we fill our minds with Jesus first, then others, joy will come to our lives. Matthew 6:33—seek first the kingdom of God... PUT GOD FIRST.

2. **Learn from Cain, Genesis 4:3-6.** He put himself first, and his countenance fell. Depression and self-pity came when he gave God the leftovers rather than giving him the first of his crops. Believe this: giving and tithing is good emotional medicine!

3. **Take advantage of the feelings of self-pity.** How? Recognize those as reminders that OTHER people are suffering. Find someone suffering more than you, and do something for them (Matthew 9:13).

4. **Recognize self-pity is actually doing the opposite to you.** Its destroying you rather than comforting you. ASK the Holy Spirit to comfort you (John 14:16).

5. **And believe in the Father's love** Psalm 103:13. Just as a father has compassion on his children, so the Lord has compassion and pity upon them that

fear Him. Remember the definition of fear: devoted focus. Devote your focus to God, and His pity and compassion will fill your heart, leaving no room for self-pity.

6. **Accept your acceptance with God.** Resist REJECTION—You are accepted in the beloved (Ephesians 1:6, Mark 1:11).

THINK IT & SAY IT

I put God first in my life, and my countenance is LIFTED! When I feel low, I will be sensitive to the needs of others and encourage them. I believe in the Father's love, and accept His acceptance in my life. I resist rejection and feelings of self-pity, in Jesus' Name!

Day 28
"Why Me?"

Today we're fasting from the thought that says, "Why me?"
When something doesn't go our way, its easy to feel sorry
for ourselves AND to feel that God and life are not fair. And
while life isn't always fair, God will always be good to you!

CHANGE IT TODAY

1. **Prepare your mind for battle.** The devil wants you to
   question yourself and question God. 1 Timothy 6:12
   says, "Fight the good fight of faith". You win the battle
   when you hold on to God's Word no matter what
   happens to you or around you.

2. **Recognize you're a target of the enemy.** Satan
   REALIZES how powerful you are, so he tries to bring
   affliction and persecution to steal the Word from your
   heart (Mark 4:15).

3. **Refuse to feel guilty when things don't go your way.**
   Stop beating yourself up and blaming yourself. Its
   not about 'what's wrong with you' or 'why you're
   being picked on.' You are a threat to the kingdom of
   darkness, which makes you a high value target.

4. **Know your authority.** YOU HAVE POWER OVER THE
   ENEMY (Luke 10:19). Submit to God (and His Word),
   resist the devil, and he will flee (James 4:7).

5. **Believe in the power of God's intervention.** Genesis
   50:20—what was meant for evil, God will turn to
   good. We'll stop asking "why" and "why me", when
   we TRUST God. He can turn any situation around if we
   surrender it to Him.

6. Fix your eyes on Jesus (Hebrews 12:2). He will finish what He started in your life. And get the focus off YOU and on HIM. Joy and confidence will come from that.

THINK IT & SAY IT

I will fight the fight of faith by holding on to the Word of God. I have authority over the devil and his guilt, and I resist him with the Word of God. I expect God to turn my situation around, and I will not act like the victim. I am more than a conqueror and my eyes are on Him, in Jesus' Name.

Day 29
"I Don't Like Myself."

Today we're fasting from the thought that says: "I don't like myself."

Thoughts on this family tree include: "I don't like the way I act, the way I look, my life, my personality, etc." This kind of self-derision and self-condemnation defeats us before we ever face our day. It causes poor self-worth, limited expectations, bad decisions and bad habits.

CHANGE IT TODAY

1. **You care for and improve what you VALUE.** Let's learn to value ourselves.

2. **You are valuable.** The value of a thing is determined by how much someone would pay for that thing. God paid for you with the blood of Jesus (Revelation 1:5, Acts 20:28). That makes you special and costly. Believe that.

3. **You are amazing!** Meditate on the truth that you are fearfully and WONDERFULLY made (Psalm 139:14). You were made to resemble God (Genesis 1:26).

4. **Meditate on your new self.** "Created to be like God in true righteousness and holiness" (Ephesians 4:24).

5. **The Holy Spirit lives in you!** (1 Corinthians 3:16). He could have chosen to live anywhere, but He chose YOU. He likes you. So you need to like you.

6. Keep looking at the Bible as a mirror. As you do, you will be transformed into that image (2 Corinthians 3:16-17). Meditating on God's Word IS changing you into the person that is impossible not to like!

THINK IT & SAY IT

I have value. God paid for me with His own blood. He has made me to resemble Him on the inside, and as I meditate on this truth, I will start to look like Him in my everyday life, as well. The Holy Spirit lives in me, and is transforming me into a person impossible not to like, in Jesus' Name.

Day 30

"I'm Ruined. I've Messed Things Up Too Badly."

Today we're fasting from the thought that says, "I'm ruined." "I've messed things up too badly." "My mistakes are too great."

This thinking goes beyond feeling guilty. It reminds us of our failures, robbing us of creativity, initiative, and the power to live in God's fullness.

CHANGE IT TODAY

1. **Believe, with every fiber of your heart and mind, in the MERCY of God (Hebrews 4:15-16).** A woman asked Napoleon to have mercy on her son, who was about to be hanged. "Do you realize the crimes he's committed against France, madam? He doesn't deserve merc," Napoleon answered. She responded, "If he deserved it, it wouldn't be mercy, Emperor." At that, the man was set free.

2. **Don't underestimate the power of confession** (1 John 1:9). Confessing our sins before God is both liberating and therapeutic. He is faithful to forgive, to cleanse and to heal (James 5:16).

3. **Do not allow your multiple mistakes DEFINE you.** No matter how bad you've messed up, get up and live another day (Proverbs 24:16).

4. **See the silver lining. You HAVE become smarter.** You ARE better. Your maturity and experience are going to show up in MORE important things ahead. Trust the work of God in you. Philippians 2:13 says, "God is at work in you, to will and work for His good pleasure."

5. **Think like a winner.** Romans 8:37 says you are more than a conqueror—no matter how far you've fallen, failed, or messed up, YOU ARE MORE THAN A CONQUEROR.

6. **Accept that God has not stopped loving you or believing in you** (Romans 8:38-39). Nothing can separate you from His Love. Nothing past, present or TO COME!

THINK IT & SAY IT

There is now NO condemnation to me, because I am in Christ. I accept God's mercy in spite of all my mistakes. I will not allow my sins or failures to define me. I am the righteousness of GOD. He is at work in me still, and nothing shall separate me from His love—making me more than a conqueror, in Jesus' Name.

Day 31

"MY LIFE IS NOT VERY SPECIAL."

Today we are fasting from the thought that says: "My life is not very special. I feel insignificant and overlooked."

Though hard to admit, this mentality is often under the surface of our lives. It's a mindset that hems us into a mediocre and boring existence. It undermines our confidence and willingness to take positive risks and stretch our faith.

CHANGE IT TODAY

1. **You have a destiny.** Believe it. Jeremiah 1:5 says, "Before you were formed in your mother's womb, I knew you and destined you..."

2. **Remember the song:** "You're just too good to be true. Can't keep my eyes off of you..." THIS IS WHAT GOD IS SAYING ABOUT YOU!!!!! Genesis 16:13a—You are the God who sees me!

3. **You cannot go unnoticed!** Luke 8:47 says, "Then, the woman, seeing that she could not go unnoticed, came trembling and fell at His feet." You are chosen by God (Colossians 3:12). HE notices you!

4. **Jesus is coming over!** Remember Zacchaeus climbing in a tree to see Jesus (Luke 19:1-10)? In verse 5, Jesus looked up and saw him and said to him, "Zacchaeus, Come down. I must stay at your house today." He wants to come to your house today. YOU ARE THAT IMPORTANT TO HIM.

5. **You are the apple of His eye.** Whoever touches you, touches the apple of God's eye (Zechariah 2:8, Psalm 17:8). You are God's greatest desire. That's why He speaks to us in our dreams (Job 33:14-16).

THINK IT & SAY IT

I have a destiny. I am chosen by God. I cannot go unnoticed by Jesus. He sees me and recognizes me, and calls me His own. He is coming over to my house, because He loves me and considers me significant. I reject all feelings of insignificance and unimportance. I am the apple of His eye, in Jesus' Name.

Day 32
I Always Seem Disappointed."

Today we're fasting from the thought that says, "I always seem disappointed." "I always feel let down."

CHANGE IT TODAY

1. **Hope in anything other than God leads to disappointment.** Psalm 43:5 says, "Why so downcast O my soul, put your hope in God." You see, putting your hope in God casts out disappointment.

2. **Expect something to praise Him about.** At the end of Psalm 43:5, David says, "For I will yet praise Him." No matter how bad it looks, something good is coming!

3. **Build your life around the promises of God.** Nothing else is certain, but His promises are (2 Corinthians 1:20).

4. **Trust the God of OPEN DOORS.** Revelation 3:8 says, "I have set before you an open door, which no one is able to shut." No matter what hasn't worked out, believe that God will open a door for you.

5. **Adopt an attitude of thanks and praise.** When God is enough, He always gives us more. Be satisfied by Him. He is El Shaddai—The God of more than enough. HE HIMSELF is more than enough.

6. **Trust HIM to give you the desires of your heart** (Psalm 37:4). He will put the right desires there; and He will fulfill them. When people disappoint you, rejoice—God will never disappoint. (Romans 5:5, Hebrews 13:5-6)

THINK IT & SAY IT

My hope is in God. No matter what, something good is coming my way FROM GOD. He will open doors, no matter how many have closed. He is more than enough for me, and I trust Him to give me the desires of my heart, in Jesus' Name.

Day 33
"I Can't Seem To Stop Worrying."

Today we're fasting from the thought that says, "I can't seem to stop worrying."

Worry is the diseased child of fear and unbelief.

CHANGE IT TODAY

1. **Expect healing from the DISEASE of worry.** Worry is a disease that spreads to physical and mental disorders (Proverbs 12:25). 1 Peter 2:24—With His stripes you were healed.

2. **USE worry as a SIGNAL to pray.** When your mind is telling you to worry, your spirit is telling you to pray! Philippians 4:6-7 says, "Don't worry about anything; instead, pray about everything. Tell God what you need, and thank Him for all He has done. Then you will experience God's peace..."

3. **Go deep with God.** Worry will leave. In Matthew 6:33 the Message Translation: "Steep your life in God... Don't worry about missing out. You'll find all your everyday concerns will be met.

4. **Meditate** on Philippians 4:13. "I can do all things through Christ which strengthens me." That includes the ability to stop worrying.

5. **Realize worry CAN'T add to your life** (Luke 12:25). When you KNOW something is taking from your life, rather than adding to it, you stop it.

THINK IT & SAY IT

I recognize worry as a disease that I AM healed from today! When worry comes to my mind, I will listen to my spirit telling me to pray. I steep my life deeply in God and I expect worry to leave. I refuse to let worry take from me another day of my life, in Jesus' Name!

Day 34

"How Could A Loving God Allow Suffering Or Evil To Happen In My Life?"

Today we're fasting from the thought that says, "How could a loving God allow suffering or evil to happen in my life or in the world?"

We've all had these thoughts run through our mind. This is a mentality that robs us of the sheer delight of enjoying the most beautiful Being in the universe. Any doubts of His goodness will lead to low and negative expectations.

CHANGE IT TODAY

1. **Believe in the goodness of God.** James 1:17 says, "Every GOOD and perfect gift comes from God." Anything that is not good or perfect is not from God.

2. **He is touched by our feelings and infirmities (Hebrews 4:15).** No one is touched as deeply with humanity's pain and anguish more than our Heavenly Father. Our sorrow and suffering aches the heart of God. He weeps with us, and offers His mercy and grace in time of need (Hebrews 4:16).

3. **Change the way you look at love.** LOVE gives free will. If God forced everyone to do right, it would be slavery. Life would become meaningless, and there would be no virtue if it were forced virtue, no honor if it was forced honor, no love if it were forced love

(Deuteronomy 30:19). Suffering was born when man chose to disbelieve and disobey God (Genesis 2:16-17).

4. **Join Paul in believing that no evil can separate us from the love of God** (Romans 8:39). Though we don't understand everything, our trust is in His love. "Knowing God" is better than "knowing why". (Of course, that doesn't mean that we just accept whatever happens in life. We have authority to make right choices, to exercise our God-given rights.)

5. **Understand God's patience.** If God wiped out everyone who ever caused pain by selfishness, lying, hatred, anger, or cheating, who would be left? We would all be swept away. If we are sane, we don't want justice. We want and need mercy! James 2:14—Mercy triumphs over judgment.

6. **Believe** that, though God doesn't cause evil, He can still bring good in the midst of evil or suffering (Genesis 50:20).

THINK IT & SAY IT

I believe in the goodness of God. He is ALWAYS good. He feels AND bears my pain. His love gives me the power of choice, and I choose to believe Him and honor Him. And no matter what, nothing can separate me from His love. His mercy triumphs over evil, and I believe He can bring good in the midst of any bad situation, in Jesus' Name!

Day 35

"LIFE IS SUCH A MYSTERY. I CAN'T SEEM TO FIGURE IT ALL OUT."

Today, we're fasting from the thought that says: "Life is such a mystery. I can't seem to figure it all out."

Life will remain a frustration and a mystery until we know the heart of God.

CHANGE IT TODAY

1. **See yourself yoked to Jesus.** Jesus said, "My yoke is easy and my burden is light" (Matthew 11:29). This means we are ATTACHED to Him. When we don't know where we're going or have to strength to get there, He continues to plow forward, bringing us with Him.

2. **Discover the mysteries of His LOVE.** THEN, and only THEN, will you discover the mysteries of this LIFE (Song of Solomon 1:2).

3. **Life will always be a mystery and frustrating until we KNOW the Word of God.** God doesn't work in mysterious ways. He works according to His Word. Learn His Word, and you will truly live (Deuteronomy 8:3).

4. **Recognize the Holy Spirit is in you** (1 Corinthians 3:16) If you are born again, He lives in you. This is how you know the heart of God. John 16:13 says He will reveal to you things to come.

5. **Pray in the Holy Spirit.** As you pray the Word, and pray in tongues, you unfold and solve the mysteries of life (1 Corinthians 14:1-2; 1 John 5:14-15).

6. **Ask Him to reveal** to you the things that eye has not seen, and ear has not heard (1 Corinthians 2:9-10)! That's what the Holy Spirit does!

THINK IT & SAY IT

I am yoked to Jesus, and He will bring me forward into God's will and purpose. I know the heart of God by knowing that the Holy Spirit lives in me. I yield myself to the Spirit of God and to the Word of God. I expect Him to reveal to me the things to come and prepare me for anything and everything, in Jesus' Name.

Day 36

"FASTING FROM THOUGHTS OF DOUBT"

Today we're fasting from thoughts of doubt, and attacking "doubt" with our faith. "I doubt that could happen." "No way!", etc.

Jesus said, "Why did you doubt?" (Matthew 14:31). Clearly, He believes in us and in our ability to be free from doubt.

CHANGE IT TODAY

1. **Discover the root of doubt.** Doubt comes when we judge our situation by what it looks like or what we feel, rather than by what God said (2 Corinthians 5:7).

2. **Understand the meaning.** Doubt means DOUBLE, to be divided in your mind. We must CHOOSE to believe ONLY the Word of God.

3. **Recognize the consequence of doubt** (James 1:6-7). The one who doubts CAN'T receive from God.

4. **Starve your doubt.** When the thought of doubt comes, replace it with the exact opposite thought. For example, if the thought comes: "I'm not sure I can overcome this." Replace it immediately with: "I am more than a conqueror, more than an overcomer through Him who loves me" (Romans 8:37).

5. **Be child-like.** Don't over-analyze. A child does not doubt. You never hear 3-or 4-year olds say, "No way." They haven't let reason, intellect and life experiences dampen their faith. See yourself as a child—A child of God. Accept what He says, and get rid of the "no way's."

6. Purify yourself in a NEW way. It's not about purifying from all wrong behaviors. It's purifying from all doubt— washing ourselves with the pure water of Gods promises (Ephesians 5:26).

THINK IT & SAY IT

I attack doubt today by choosing to believe what God says, regardless of what I see or feel. I will not be of those who don't receive from God. I feed my faith with the Word and starve my doubts. I reject the reasonings and logic that contradict the Word and I read the promises of God to wash my mind and heart of all doubt, in Jesus' Name!

Day 37

"FASTING FROM DOUBT, PART II!"

Today, we are continuing to fast from thoughts of Doubt.

When Jesus asked Peter, "Why did you doubt?", He was revealing to us that it's unnatural to doubt, and we were born to believe!

CHANGE IT TODAY

1. **See doubt and unbelief for what it is.** It is deception. The devil is attempting to deceive us into THINKING 3 things: a.) that God's Word won't work; b.) that God isn't good; and c.) that we don't have authority over the devil.

2. **True knowledge drives out doubt.** True knowledge is not what you learn in college. True knowledge is what God said and told us HE WOULD DO. Awaken to the knowledge of God's promises, and doubt will begin to die.

3. **Remember. Remember.** Psalm 103:2 says to forget none of His benefits. It blesses God when you remember what He's already done. Remembering what He's done makes you thankful. And thankfulness is the highest form of faith. Faith doesn't say, "Will you?" Faith says, "Thank you!" Remember, and your faith will soar!

4. **Eliminate Passivity.** We must not tolerate doubt in our hearts. Proverbs 4:23 says, "Watch over your heart with ALL DILIGENCE..." Refuse to accept the lie that "we all doubt." Doubts do come, but we must drive them out.

5. **Go back to the garden** (Genesis 2:15). Adam's life was destroyed because he didn't drive out doubt from the garden of Eden. When we question God's Word, we open the door to doubt, unbelief and the devil. SHUT THE DOOR. How? Fill your mind and heart with the promises of God.

6. **Give up gambling!** What do I mean? Believing anything OTHER than God's Word is a gamble. Only His promises are a sure thing. 2 Corinthians 1:20—all the promises of God are YES. 1 Kings 8:56 says, "Not one Word has failed of ALL His good promise."

THINK IT & SAY IT

I declare that God's Word works, that God IS good, and that I have authority over the devil. I drive out the devil from the garden of my heart by driving doubt out. I believe God cannot lie, and that every promise He makes comes to pass. I refuse to accept doubt another day in my life, in Jesus' Name

Day 38
FAST FROM NEGATIVITY!

Today we're fasting from NEGATIVITY! So many people look at things in a negative way, expect negative things to happen, and speak themselves into negative results.

CHANGE IT TODAY

1. **God is a positive God.** 2 Corinthians 1:20 says "All the promises of God are YES!" John 15:7 says, "If you abide in Me, and My words abide in you, ask whatever you wish, and it will be done for you."

2. **Believe in the possibilities.** Chauncy M. Depew warned his nephew not to invest $5,000 in Ford Automobile stock because nothing could come along that would be better than the horse! Mark 9:23 says, "All things are possible to him who believes!"

3. **CAN IT!** Success comes in "CANS," not in "cannots!" Philippians 4:13 says, "I CAN do all things through Christ which strengthens me."

4. **Get rid of the NEGATIVE PSYCHIC in you.** 'The negative psychic' in you presumes you know what people are thinking about you. "She thinks I'm an idiot." "I can tell he's always judging me.", etc. The only person's thoughts that matter about you are God's and THEY ARE GOOD (Psalm 139:17-18).

5. **Stop seeing giants.** And see yourself as the giant. Begin to see yourself conquering everything! (Numbers 13:30; Romans 8:37)

6. **DECIDE TODAY** that you are leaving negative thinking behind, and begin to express your God-given positive and victorious mentality in EVERYTHING (Genesis 1:26). You are made in His image, and He looks at everything from a winning point of view.

IT'S NOT TOO LATE TO SEE YOURSELF DIFFERENTLY!

THINK IT & SAY IT

I declare that I can do all things through Christ which strengthens me! All things are possible and all things are going to work in my favor. I believe God's thoughts toward me are supernaturally GOOD. And I leave behind negative thinking beginning today, in Jesus' Name!

Day 39

"FASTING FROM THOUGHTS OF FAILURE AND DEFEAT."

Today, we're fasting from thoughts of failure and defeat.

From this day forward, we are adopting a VICTORY mindset. We are giving up and abstaining from EVERY thought of defeat or failure.

CHANGE IT TODAY

1. **You are MADE TO WIN.** Get this in your thinking. You are a winner. "You are the head and not the tail; you shall be above ONLY, and not underneath" (Deuteronomy 28:13). Notice the word ONLY. You are ONLY going to be above, on top, victorious.

2. **Meditate on God's promise:** "Everything you put your hand to WILL prosper" (Deuteronomy 28:8). Fill your mind with this thought. Expect to prosper. Expect to succeed. Expect to have victory.

3. **Even bad can turn into good.** Remember Romans 8:28 says "All things work together for good, to those who love God and are called according to His purpose."

4. **Expect the tables to turn!** Esther 9:1 says, "On that day, their enemies had hoped to overpower them, IT WAS TURNED TO THE CONTRARY; and the Jews overpowered those who hated them." In the Message translation, it says: "This was the very day, the tables were now turned!" In the day of certain defeat, God turned it into total victory. And if He did it for them, He will do it for you (Galatians 3:29)!

5. **Believe in the power of Jesus' prayer.** In Luke 22:32, Jesus said to Peter (and to YOU) "I have prayed for you, that your faith would not fail." He gets His prayers **answered! Amen? YOU'RE NOT GOING TO FAIL!**

6. **Add this ingredient to every attitude, event and circumstance of life: FAITH** (1 John 5:4). This is the VICTORY, that overcomes the world, even our FAITH.

THINK IT & SAY IT

I will never be defeated another day in my life. I am redeemed from failure and defeat. I am the head and not the tail. Everything I put my hand to will succeed and prosper. No matter what is against me, I expect the tables to turn to my favor. My faith will not fail, because Jesus is praying for it! Amen!

Day 40
"WILL GOD DO IT?"

Today we're fasting from the thought that says, "Will God do it?" So often, we question whether or not God will answer our prayer, whether or not He will heal, whether or not He will deliver or rescue us... We need to put an end to this thinking that blocks our faith and blocks God's power.

CHANGE IT TODAY:

1. **Always start thinking about anything with A PROMISE FROM GOD'S WORD:** Psalm 37:5—"Commit your way to the Lord; trust also in Him, and He will bring it to pass."

2. **THINK HIS WAY, AND DO THINGS HIS WAY** (Psalm 37:5). Commit to thinking His thoughts and following His system—His way of doing things (i.e. sowing/reaping, forgiving, love, faith, trust, etc.)

3. **Know He has called you.** You may not be "called" to be a minister, but you are "called" to receive God's promises and purpose for your life! (1 Thessalonians 5:24 - The one who CALLED you is FAITHFUL, and HE WILL DO IT!)

4. **Turn your concerns over to Him.** Psalm 138:8 says, "He will accomplish (fulfill) what concerns me."

5. **Be convinced** He does what He promises to do. Isaiah 46:11 says, "...yea, I have spoken it, I will also bring it to pass..."

6. **Think: Possibility!!!!** In Mark 9:23, Jesus said, "All things are possible to those who believe."

7. **It's already DONE.** Meditate on the last 3 words Jesus spoke before He died: IT is FINISHED (John 19:30)! His death established God's covenant of promise to you. It's done. Believe it.

THINK IT & SAY IT

I declare my God is faithful to do what He promised in my life. He will fulfill His promises which include saving, healing, restoring and blessing me. He is the same yesterday, today and forever. Jesus did it all on the cross. IT is FINISHED. HE has already provided for my every need, in Jesus' Name.

Conclusion

Now that you've begun this LASTING CHANGE From the Inside Out, let me encourage you with a few final thoughts.

1. **Review regularly.** Don't let up. Life will try to pull you back into wrong thinking. Whenever a negative thought comes back, go back and review how to overcome this thought from that particular day.

2. **Share your testimony.** Something else that will keep you walking in victory is sharing how God has changed your life. Please send me your testimony at www.thinkingfast.org. This will encourage someone else to know that their life can be changed too!

3. **Help me take this revolution to the world.** God has called us to change the world, one life at a time, one thought at a time. You can help me take this revolutionary message to millions of others around the world by sowing a seed of change in others. Just log onto www.thinkingfast.org and click on "Make a Donation." Stand with me in getting the word out about this life-changing fast from wrong thinking.

4. **Finally, don't ever forget:** There is no stopping the man or woman who is set free from wrong thinking. Remember, "As a man thinks within, so is he!" (Proverbs 23:7)